If you have (...
for what to say to ...
you will see why people asked for ...

Text by Lois Rock
Text copyright © 1996 Lion Publishing
Illustrations copyright © 1996 Roger Langton

Published by
Lion Publishing plc
Sandy Lane West, Littlemore, Oxford, England
ISBN 0 7459 3104 9
Albatross Books Pty Ltd
PO Box 320, Sutherland, NSW 2232, Australia
ISBN 0 7324 0964 0

First edition 1996
10 9 8 7 6 5 4 3 2 1 0

A catalogue record for this book
is available from the British Library

Printed and bound in Singapore

**This retelling is based on the stories
of Jesus' life in the Bible.**

Jesus' Special Prayer

Retold by Lois Rock
Illustrations by Roger Langton

A LION BOOK

Jesus always welcomed people who wanted to see him.

He always seemed to have time for them.

Jesus always spent time with God, too. Sometimes he got up early and went for a walk in the hills by himself.

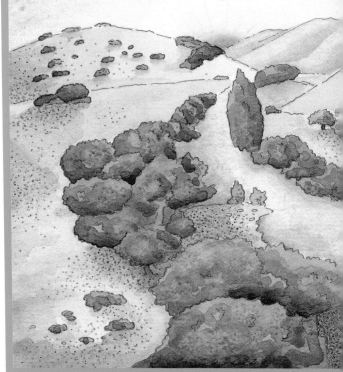

There he talked to God and listened to God: Jesus spent time praying.

Sometimes when he wanted to pray, he stayed in a room, quietly, by himself, with the door closed.

"Some people like to pray in a place where everyone will see them," Jesus told his friends. "They are happy just because other people notice how much they pray.

"But you must go somewhere where no one will notice you. Pray to God just as you talk to a father who really loves you. God will hear your prayers."

"What shall we say in our prayers?" asked Jesus' friends.

"A short prayer is fine," said Jesus. "God knows what you really want to say anyway. So, pray like this:

"Dear Father God
you are greater than anything
in this world.
You are everything that is
good and right.

"I want everyone in the world
to know how great you are,
so they will treat you as their king
and live as you want.

"Please give us the things we need for living today.

"Forgive us the wrong things
we have done,
as we forgive other people who
have done wrong things to us.

"Please keep us safe from anything that makes us want to forget you and disobey you, and from anything that stops us being your friends."

Then Jesus went on to say this to the
people listening:
"Ask: God will give.
Look for God: you will find God.
Knock: God will open the door
to you.

"God wants to give you good things, and to come and live as your friend always."

A Christian prayer

Our Father in heaven,
hallowed be your name,
your kingdom come,
your will be done,
on earth as in heaven.
Give us today our daily bread.
Forgive us our sins
as we forgive those who sin against us.
Lead us not into temptation
but deliver us from evil.
For the kingdom, the power, and the
glory are yours now and for ever.
Amen.